TAKE CHARGE!

A RAPID-ACCESS MANAGEMENT PRIMER for the professional, this quality reference book is designed to provide business people who've moved swiftly into management positions with the knowledge and skills they need.

Experience total confidence as you run meetings, delegate authority, hire, fire, evaluate, and reward your staff. Create the kind of optimal working environment that produces results and wins respect.

Whether you're dealing with a professional office, service agency, small office, or multinational corporation—you can learn how to be an effective boss. Here are the proven skills, techniques, and insider's information essential for winning a competitive edge in today's fast-paced business world.

BEING

— A —

BOSS

Cheryl Reimold

A DELL BOOK

Published by
Dell Publishing
a division of
The Bantam Doubleday Dell
Publishing Group, Inc.
666 Fifth Avenue
New York, New York 10103

To
IW

ISBN: 0-440-20193-4
Reprinted by arrangement with Cloverdale Press, Inc.

Printed in the United States of America
Published simultaneously in Canada
One Previous Dell Trade Edition
July 1988
10 9 8 7 6 5 4 3 2 1
OPM

Contents

CONTENTS

Preface

I am going to show you how to be a good boss —and love doing it.

Whether you're a sales manager, a head physician, a college president, the owner of a business, or anyone else who has to guide and manage people at work—you'll learn how, here.

For the rules are the same no matter what the profession.

First you must understand what it means "to be a boss." You must know what, exactly, you are trying to accomplish.

Then you need certain techniques for hiring the right people, delegating work, and staying in control of all the many tasks under your supervision.

Finally, to be a *great* boss, you have to be able to motivate your people to do their very best for you and for themselves.

This book will teach you how to meet all these challenges. When you've finished it, you will *know* you have your job under control. When you've put its techniques to work, you'll agree that being a boss is one of the most exciting, rewarding human efforts.

With this book you will not only learn to be a good boss. You will learn to *enjoy* it. And when you enjoy your work, you pass the pleasure on to your staff.

Enthusiasm is infectious. It works. (In fact, Management by Objectives might just be replaced by Management by Enthusiasm!)

So let's get on with passing it around. Before you turn the page, though—a word of explanation. I wrote this book so that you could read it easily and with pleasure. So I used one pronoun for both sexes, purely for readability. For *he,* read *he/she.* Until we have an androgynous pronoun in common currency, it's the clearest and simplest way!

BEING

— A —

BOSS

1

The Seven Secrets of Being a Number One Boss

Self-trust is the first secret of success.

Emerson

You are now a boss. What does that mean? A local tsar? A superstar? A coordinator? A five-star general? The expert in the field? All of the above??

WHAT IT MEANS TO BE A BOSS

One of the problems bosses have is a muddled job description. They're not quite sure what being a boss means.

Yet it's quite simple. To find out, let's imagine for a moment a company with *no* bosses.

Suppose a young writer decides to start a new magazine. He rounds up some enthusiastic friends—one to illustrate it, another to sell space for ads, and a third to take care of the financial arrangements. They agree on a schedule and prepare for the first issue.

And then the problems start. First—time. The writer finds he can't come up with ideas, research them, interview people, and write all the articles in fifteen days. The sales rep can't cover all the territory alone. The artist is dogging the footsteps of the writer and the sales rep—eager to have some material to illustrate. He gets it all two days before the final deadline. And then there's no time left to put the whole magazine together. The accountant has little to account for.

The next problem is human limitation. These four have the capacity of only four human minds and imaginations. Pretty soon, their magazine—if they ever get it out—will become stale.

Then come the problems of the inner sanctum. The four workers will quickly blame each other for not getting the magazine out on time. Further, their priorities will differ. The writer may want a magazine full of controversial articles. The artist would opt instead for pages of gorgeous pictures. And whoever has invested the most money in the venture will probably want a journal full of well-paying ads and articles that please the advertisers.

Who is to decide?

WHY BUSINESS NEEDS BOSSES

I have greatly oversimplified the difficulties. But from even this elementary scheme, you can see that these four people need both to *have* a boss and either to *be* or to *hire* departmental bosses themselves.

They need a boss to look over the whole organization and *determine its needs.* How much money do they have to put into that first issue? How many writers, illustrators, and sales reps do they need to get the issue together on time? What about office staff . . . office equipment . . . supplies . . . subscribers?

They need a boss to *coordinate all the efforts,* arranging a work plan and a detailed schedule so that each person can perform effectively and make the deadline.

They need a boss to *make the decisions* on the contents, organization, and look of the magazine.

They need a boss to take all their ideas and come up with an acceptable *goal* for their enterprise—a goal toward which they will all work.

Then, in each of their departments, they need a boss to *hire* enough specialists to get the work done well and on time. That boss will have to *keep harmony* among the different specialists so that working together increases, rather than impedes, productivity. He will have to *set an overall goal, make decisions, determine needs,* and *coordinate efforts,* just like the boss of the whole operation.

Are you beginning to see that being a boss is far more than being a coordinator? More than hiring and firing? More than giving orders and cracking the whip?

Think back to that original group of four starting a magazine. They had a lot going for them. They were all committed to the success of their venture. They were all willing to work as hard as necessary to ensure its success. Each one, alone in his field, could make decisions and act on them, without having to convince anyone else to do what he wished. Each one-man department was free of strife. The only problem was, no one person could do his whole department's work.

Realizing that they cannot put out a competitive magazine this way, they decide to change their organization. Instead of having four independent professionals, they will have a *president* in charge of the whole organization and *departmental managers* or *directors* guiding the work of the employees in each specialty. The four original workers become *bosses.* The writer, for instance, becomes editor-in-chief. He hires a staff of specialists—a sports writer or editor, a travel writer or editor, and so on. He may take on an editorial assistant. But however he staffs his department, he still wants to achieve *exactly the same results as if he were the sole person in it.*

He still wants top-quality, varied articles. He wants to inform, stimulate, and entertain his readers. He may want to formulate a certain editorial profile for the magazine. None of these fundamental goals changed when he became a boss. *All that changed was his way of working toward them.*

Instead of trying to do it all himself, he hires a team to do it with him. Instead of having only his own energy to channel, he has a number of personalities and talents to guide in the direction of those goals. And instead of having only his own brain to draw on, he has several good, creative minds bringing fresh ideas.

So, as a boss, he gains variety, creativity, new ideas, and time. But he also has to give up certain benefits—such as the ego-building pleasure of writing or commissioning all the articles himself! The giving up is not so easy, and the bad boss doesn't do it. He finds ways to keep his hand in, and builds resounding resentments in his employees as a result.

But if the writer learns to delegate (tips on learning to do this appear in a later chapter), he can achieve his ideal: to keep the efficiency and wholeness of his original one-man operation, while adding to it the extra work, imagination, and expertise of his new employees.

DIFFERENT KINDS OF BOSSES

You may be . . . a professional with one assistant; the manager of a department; the president of a company. Or somewhere in between. You're still a boss, and as such, your job—in all these positions—is substantially the same. However, your particular position in the company does affect your managerial work in three important areas. You should be aware of these.

1. Relationships. If you have one assistant reporting to you, you can focus on making your relationship with that person harmonious and productive. But if you have more than one reporting to you, you have to consider the effect your behavior to one has on the others. If you openly praise Mary and say nothing to John, you make him feel unappreciated. If you openly chastise Mary in front of John, you diminish her in his eyes. This is particularly damaging if Mary happens to be John's boss, for you rob her of her authority. The answer? Be aware of the domino effect. Guard absolutely against favoritism. And never praise or blame an employee in front of others.

2. Knowledge of your staff's work. If you have one or two people reporting to you, you know what they're doing. If you have several hundreds or thousands who report to others who report to you, you have to *make it your job to find out* what your people are doing. Otherwise you will lose control of your business.

3. Accountability. If you're the president of your own, privately held company, you're accountable to no one. You can build your own starship or dig your own grave. You don't have to explain your actions (though you would be wise to do so, if you want to keep the trust of your staff). You set the ultimate goal. You bear the ultimate responsibility.

But if you're anyone other than the president of your own company, you're accountable to someone for your actions. You have to keep this in mind when setting goals and making promises or threats. Be sure you never arrange, promise, or threaten anything that depends on somebody else's okay before you have secured that okay.

It will help to bear these differences in mind as you move from one type of bosshood to another. But you will find that you will meet the different demands perfectly, and naturally, if you remember that, as a boss, your goal is *al-*

ways group excellence, not personal aggrandizement. With this goal before you, you'll accomplish the miracle of having several or several hundred people working together as one, with no sacrifice of individuality.

Can you see that being a good boss is one of the most exciting, challenging human endeavors possible—with tremendous professional and personal rewards? Good. Then let us turn to the seven secrets that will get you there.

THE SEVEN SECRETS

1. Develop professional expertise. You must understand the work of each member of your staff very well indeed. This doesn't mean you have to be a technical expert in thirty different specialties. Nor does it mean you have to be able to do each person's job. But you *must* know:

- What each employee is doing

- How he is doing it

- What results you and he expect

- What major problems he may face

Apply these four criteria rigorously to the jobs of everyone who works for you. If you know all four, you will be competent to direct your staff with authority, to help each member with a work problem, to coordinate efforts meaningfully, and to explain to *your* superiors what's going on in your department and why. If you don't know them all, you have some critical homework to do. Talk to your subordinates. Ask them what you need to know. You're not expected to be omniscient. You *are* expected to know your employees' jobs.

If you need more technical details to cover these four criteria, get them. Round up some books and articles on the subject. Ask your colleagues to recommend some. Go to the library. Check the card catalogue listings under the subject of interest. Go through the *Readers' Guide to Periodical Literature,* plus any technical reference books that will lead you to pertinent sources of information. Once again, don't be afraid to ask for help. Remember, your job is not to *appear* all-knowing to everyone you meet. Rather, you have to acquire as much expertise as possible on all the work going on in your department. As a boss, you have far too many really important things to do to waste time worrying about appearing perfect!

2. Sharpen your communication skills. Communication occurs when one person talks or writes to another—*and the intended message is the one the listener hears.* This happens surprisingly rarely. *Interference* between speaker and listener usually deflects and confuses the message—though both people think they have communicated. Interference can be: the expression in the speaker's eyes . . . his tone of voice . . . even the words he chooses. All these can transmit powerful messages of their own, such as "I'm angry," "I doubt if you're smart enough to get this so I'll keep repeating it," or even "You're good-looking and I'd like to get to know you better off the job." The listener pays more attention to these messages than to the one intended, for they are direct, powerful, and personal.

The listener can impede communication by his *expectations.* If he expects the speaker to say certain things, he'll tend to hear those things, no matter what the speaker is actually saying.

Finally, the greatest barrier to communication lies in *different basic assumptions.* You assume the employee will do A; he thinks his job is to do B. When you upbraid him for *not* doing A, he feels so outraged at this unjustified attack that he doesn't even hear what you're saying.

How can you learn to communicate with your staff?

First, be aware of the visual and tonal messages you and others transmit. Put yourself in control of *your* side of the communication by determining *not* to send opposing or confusing messages via these channels. And concentrate on *all* the messages your employee is giving you, so as to understand what's really on his mind.

Second, realize that your employees expect you to say certain things *because you usually do say them.* If you have something unusual to say— *tell* them that you are departing from your original philosophy or demands, and that you have something new to communicate. By preparing them to expect something new, you open their ears.

Finally, you can create common basic assumptions between you by *setting careful job descriptions and goals* at the outset of your work together.

Your written job description for each employee would define clearly:

1. the job's *specific contributions* to the company and departmental goals

2. the employee's *specific responsibilities*—what is expected of him each day, each week, each quarter, each year

3. the employee's *accountabilities*—which decisions he can make without reporting to you . . . which decisions he can make, followed by a report to you . . . and which decisions he must bring to you, with no action on his part

We'll discuss goal-setting in detail in a later chapter. For now, remember that you and your employee must agree completely on the goals toward which he is working. You can do so easily by *making his main goal the same as yours.* That shared goal is, very simply, *contribution to the company purpose.*

You begin by defining the company purpose. For example, it might be: "To be the leader in making, selling, and servicing swimming pools in the greater New York area." Then see where your job and your employee's job contribute to this effort. Define the *critical tasks* that you and your employee can pursue to this end. By following this course, you will have set a common goal that you both accept and understand—*and* you will have made the employee aware of his definite company worth.

There is another side to communication, however. Not all the messages you send will be easy—or positive. There will be times in your work as boss when your task will be to communicate to a staff member what he did wrong. (If you are a good boss this will probably not happen very often—but it will happen.)

When the occasion arises, be sure to discuss the problem with your subordinate as soon as possible after you become aware of the unsatisfactory performance. If you are to communicate clearly, you must make it clear that you are upset with his *performance,* not with *him.* Finally, show him that your purpose is to find a solution, to help him determine how to avoid a recurrence of the problem.

3. Cultivate enthusiasm. Enthusiasm is infectious. If you enjoy your work and believe in its validity, you transmit that attitude to your staff. You give them something good to work for. But if you see this job as merely a stepping-stone to positions of greater power, they will know it. And resent it. Such an attitude says, this work is worth nothing in itself. All I want is high visibility, so that I can rocket up to where the action is. How would you feel about working for a boss who thought like that? Would he be likely to inspire you to do *your* best?

To be a good boss who leads a winning team, you must love the work you're doing now. As their leader, you can give your staff the same spirit. Genuine excitement generates a response. Your people will learn from you why the work is worth doing and will then derive meaning from it themselves. And people work to have meaning, as well as money, in their lives. Don't ever forget that.

4. Keep an open mind. Too many new managers think that being a boss means being an autocrat. To see how wrong this idea is, think of your own reaction to different bosses you've had. How have you felt about the mini-tsar—the self-proclaimed emperor who rules by fear and punishment (both psychological and professional)? Everyone's had or seen such a boss at work. They abound. At first, they may seem to get results. People will follow orders out of fear—if they've got no choice. But business is not a prison camp. People can and do leave a tsar-boss. And for the period that they remain under his control, they do what they have to do to escape his punishment—but no more. He doesn't inspire them to want to do the best they can and to *enjoy* doing it. He makes work hateful.

Think back to the model of the four men who started the magazine. Remember what they gained by becoming bosses and working with a team. Among other benefits, each now had many good minds focused on the job. None of the four had to be limited by his own thoughts or capabilities. They and their magazine could profit from the ideas, suggestions, and proposals for improvement made by their staff. Yet so many bosses *don't listen.* And they lose.

They lose the real possibility of improving their work by using a better method. They are literally throwing away one of the major assets they have acquired at considerable effort and expense.

And they lose the willingness and enthusiasm of their staff. People need to feel needed. You do, don't you? Would you work hard if you knew you were considered completely dispensable? Would you try to come up with imaginative, inventive solutions to problems if you knew your boss wouldn't even listen to them? Would you?

Keep an open mind. Listen to the suggestions made by your staff, consider them seriously, and be ready to adopt them if they seem good. You, your staff, and your work will all feel the benefits.

5. Pay attention to accomplishment. Be a ready rewarder. Adults, as well as children, need to be appreciated. They need to feel that it's worth putting some extra effort into their work. You show them your appreciation by rewarding a job well done.

Rewards are not to be confused with raises—though raises are certainly one type of reward. But financial rewards are of necessity limited. You can't give someone a raise every time he does a particularly fine job. If you do, the raise will be so pitifully small that it looks ridiculous. Furthermore, such behavior is reminiscent of rewarding Fido with a bone. It's unimaginative and implies that the employee works only for money. Which he may have to do if you set things up that way.

A recent survey of management trainees found that young professionals considered *attention to accomplishment* one of the most important qualities of a working place. Other job attributes that they sought were *flexibility* and *independence.* These goals have nothing to do with money. Yet they give you opportunities to reward your workers in significant, nonfinancial ways.

We'll look at specific types of nonfinancial rewards in a later chapter, when we discuss "psychic income" and "freedom rewards." For now, just keep in mind the concept of rewarding good work. Even a smile and a handshake will make your employee feel appreciated. When you show him that his work is meaningful to you, you make it meaningful to him too. And you encourage him to want to do it well.

6. Be accessible to your staff. Always have time for every staff member. *Always.* No matter what your deadlines or how busy you happen to be. As a professional, your first interest may be your work. But as a boss, your first responsibility is to the members of your staff. They absolutely need to know that, if they are to trust you and work hard for your goals.

Practically any office problem can be alleviated by easy access to the boss. People see you as the decision maker, the arbitrator. If they're having difficulties among themselves or with their work, they need to know that they can come to you to help resolve them. Just that knowledge, that you are always there for them, will increase the chances of harmony in the office and an honest dialogue between you and the people who work for you.

7. Respect your staff. For a boss, the golden rule is: *Treat your staff as you would your clients.* You know the slogans. "Have it *your* way." "Our business is your business." "We do it all for you." They're all part of the nationwide effort of companies to woo customers. Corporations have learned that they depend on satisfied clients for their own profit and success. People do *not* settle for less these days. They go elsewhere.

This fact has penetrated the corporate consciousness. What top executives have not always realized is its sequel: To have satisfied clients, you need a committed, well-trained, hard-working staff. If people keep leaving and new trainees keep starting, the company and its clients are going to suffer a loss of quality and consistency, not to mention the financial burden of turnover. If employees are disgruntled, or simply unmotivated, they won't put themselves out for the clients, no matter what slogan the advertising department is singing. Your staff is your *most valuable asset.* Once you realize that, *really* realize it, you will treat your employees properly.

You'll treat them like clients, with respect. With concern. You'll be willing to meet them halfway on a ticklish problem. You won't let them rule you, any more than you would a customer, but neither will you assume that any one of them is easy to replace. Your attitude toward every member of your staff will say simply: You're important to me. I'm important to you. Let's do the best we can for each other.

The seven secrets of being a number one boss are:

1. **Develop professional expertise**
2. **Sharpen your communication skills**
3. **Cultivate enthusiasm**
4. **Keep an open mind**
5. **Pay attention to accomplishment**
6. **Be accessible to your staff**
7. **Respect your staff**

Cut the list out and hang it up where you can see it every day. Pretty soon, you'll see the magic at work.

2
How to Have Authority

Be swift to hear, slow to speak, slow to wrath.

James 1:19

Your first job as a boss is not to hire or to fire, to set objectives, or to run projects. Your job begins the minute anyone sees or speaks to you. The job is: to have authority.

You must be perceived as one who has the inherent right and capabilities to be a boss.

Authority is an intangible, ineffable quality, but you know it when you see it. Somebody walks into a room full of people—and all those people are somehow subtly changed. They're now focused on the newcomer. They're waiting for him to do or say something that will determine their next move or mode of behavior. He has literally taken charge. Before he says a word, he has established his undeniable authority.

Many people believe that authority comes as a natural consequence of a new title or acknowledged expertise. When a person is promoted to an executive rank, we even say he "occupies a position of authority." But the truth is, authority has very little to do with official titles. You can have it whatever your professional status. And you can lack it as the president of the company.

Can you "get" authority? Absolutely. Once you understand *what* it is and *how* to exert it.

GETTING THE FEELING

Authority is a combination of knowledge, confidence in self and others, and the ability to communicate that knowledge and confidence. You exert authority when people believe you know what you are doing and what they should do.

How do you do it?

First, by feeling it.

You must feel, really believe, that you have the knowledge, experience, intelligence, and maturity required to give direction to other people. You can get this feeling in three steps.

Step 1. Have a little humility. The people who selected you to be boss and those who chose to work for you must have some reason to believe in your ability to manage. Be humble enough to agree with them!

Step 2. Learn everything you possibly can

about your work, your people, and their work. The next chapter will show you how.

Step 3. Tell yourself three things:

1. I know enough to guide other people.

2. I believe in myself.

3. I believe in them.

Repeating those words on a basis of knowledge will give you the feeling. Try it. Regularly. Out loud. You may be surprised at its effect.

Next, you have to *radiate* that feeling of confidence and goodwill in all your behavior. I'm going to give you some techniques for achieving *physical* expression of confidence and authority. First, though, you have to feel it. Otherwise you'll look like an actor playing a part he doesn't understand.

CULTIVATING DELIBERATION

To begin, *practice deliberation.* Quick speech and movements communicate nervousness. You may be on your way to feeling good and confident—but your habits of speech and movement may be so deeply ingrained that they express a tension you don't feel. Or—you may still feel nervous! Either way, deliberate speech and movement will calm you and give you poise. Practice speaking more *slowly, distinctly,* and *softly.* Make every movement of your body a complete one. Don't half-raise your arm and then pull it back. Raise it—then let it fall. Or don't raise it at all. Think of your gestures as tracing whole geometric shapes. Don't leave one unfinished. By making complete gestures, you will feel more complete, connected, in control. That's how you have to feel if you want to have authority.

Avoid all staccato movements—tapping your feet or hands, blinking your eyes, drumming your fingers. These movements say: *I'm nervous. I'm not in control.* If you feel nervous, take deep, slow breaths. Get up and walk, slowly. Do some leisurely stretches. Even just stretching your fingers and toes at your desk will help. You will be amazed how your changed patterns of movement will improve your patterns of thought and the reactions of other people.

THE BODY LANGUAGE OF AUTHORITY

Become aware of body language. Your own and other people's. If you are explaining something important to your staff, trying to convey some of your own urgency and enthusiasm, you'll diminish your effect if you're sitting rigidly, drawn tight together, with arms and legs crossed. Your body is saying: *I'm tense, insecure, and unapproachable. I'm not sure of what I'm doing . . . and I'm certainly not sure of you.* No matter what your voice says.

And people react powerfully to visual impressions.

The body language that expresses confidence and authority is the easy, open stance, accompanied by direct eye contact with the other person. It says: *This is who I am. I have nothing to hide (so I'm not crouching into myself) . . . and I feel good about myself and you. (If I didn't feel good about you, I wouldn't be facing you easily, with no defenses up.)*

If you've been cowering, crouching, and slouching all your life, this new, forthright carriage will be difficult for you. For one thing, you'll be using muscles that haven't been called on in years! But try it. Alone in your room, sit or stand proudly, *feeling good about yourself and other people.* I guarantee you'll soon sense a kind of glow. That's the glow that accompanies authority. The difference between the person with genuine authority and the tyrant, by the way, is that the tyrant feels good *only* about himself. (Sometimes he feels just the opposite —but that's another story.)

Here's a technique to get you started in your new stance. Think of someone you admire, whose physical appearance is not wholly dissimilar to yours. Then, when you're alone, imagine you inhabit that person's body. Imagine that when people look at you, they see that spectacular individual. You'll find you carry yourself with pride and pleasure. And that's exactly how you should be walking and sitting and standing, *always.* If you find yourself slipping back into a slouch one day—remember how you felt when you "played the star." And bring the stance back. The feeling will follow.

After you've practiced this for a while and you *know* the right feeling and the right bearing, take a look in the mirror. Could you improve your appearance? Lose weight . . . gain weight . . . change your hairstyle . . . change the way you dress . . . get more exercise? If so, do what needs to be done with the firm idea that you are making something good even better.

Finally, think about what your body language is saying to people. If you walk into someone's office and go right up to his desk, your body has said: *I'm your equal.* If you stand at the edge of the doorway, your body has said: *You are in a position to dictate to me, I don't dare approach you in your sanctum.*

If you stand up to address a seated person, you gain height and a certain amount of temporary power. But if you face the person directly, on his level (whether sitting or standing), you are more likely to establish communication.

MASTERING NONVERBAL MESSAGES

You will have more control of a situation if you can read the other person's body language. If someone's fidgeting or swinging a crossed leg, he's telling you he's uneasy. Be aware of that message, and speak to it by adopting a calm, reassuring attitude. On the other hand, if a person is clearly withdrawing into his private self—looking down, tightening up, minimizing eye contact—he may be telling you one of a number of things. He may be saying: *Go away. I need to be by myself.* Or: *I'm scared of you. I'm afraid you'll take advantage of my vulnerability if I open up to you at all.* Or: *There's something I should tell you—but I don't want to. If I shield myself from contact with you, maybe I can keep it to myself.* Or some other message. As a skilled, sensitive communicator, you must not make snap judgments. Test each of the possible messages by listening to the person's words and his tone of voice. Then try gently responding to each of the messages. You'll feel the connection when you touch the right one.

As you become aware of other people's body

language, you will learn how to reach them. If a person is tense and tied up, you can approach him with very open, relaxed gestures. By complementing his *negative* attitude with your *positive* one, you may loosen him up and predispose him to listen to you. If he doesn't change but simply gets tighter, then he really wants or needs to be left alone. Leave him alone, graciously. Respect his needs—and he'll respect you.

Similarly, if a person strikes a threatening or aggressive attitude, look for its positive complement. An easy, friendly attitude gives him nothing to aggress. If he's smart, he'll calm down and meet you at the negotiating table. If he's dumb, he'll continue to roar into the night. That's his problem, not yours. He hasn't brought you down with him.

Above all—concentrate on being a power of example. Work as willingly and as hard as you want other people to work. The exhilaration and feeling of accomplishment you will derive will actually give you a deep sense of authority, which will generate naturally authoritative behavior.

Don't try to impress people with your stance or gestures. Just try to make them easy, open, and harmonious. Be committed to your work, not to your appearance of authority, and your face and body will animate your words. Believe in yourself, your work, and your employees—and let it show.

3
How to Run a Project

*Our belief at the beginning of a doubtful undertaking is
the first thing that insures the successful outcome
of the venture.*

William James

Now that you understand the concept of authority and have begun to feel its glow, you're ready to run any project. Running a project is really putting authority into action. You prepare your project in two phases.

Phase one is to get all the knowledge you need to run the project with complete confidence and understanding. You do this in five steps.

FIVE STEPS TO GETTING THE KNOWLEDGE YOU NEED

Step 1. Map out the project for yourself. Circle any areas where you feel uncertain.
Step 2. Research your files and other sources of background information to fill in the gaps.
Step 3. Set up pre-project conferences with

those involved, and don't be afraid to ask questions on subjects about which you are still unsure.

Step 4. Go over the project from the point of view of each of your staff members. Ask the questions they might ask. And answer them.

Step 5. When you feel comfortably secure in your knowledge, present it to your boss or an expert in the field to see if you've got anything wrong.

Each of these steps is a deliberate effort to increase your knowledge of the facts you need to supervise this project. As you complete each one, you will *feel* your understanding grow. By the end of all five, you will not only have the knowledge you need—you'll also be very aware that you have it. With that awareness comes confidence in yourself. You *know* you're qualified to manage the project and make the final decisions.

Furthermore, you will have increased confidence in your team. Step 4 lets you see the project from each worker's vantage point. Once you have put yourself in his position, you will know just what he has to do and how best to explain it to him. By setting these limits, you will come to feel that the task is feasible; you and he can handle it together.

You're in command of the subject. You feel confident in yourself and your staff. Now you have to be able to *communicate* that confidence. You're ready for phase two—communication.

FIVE GUIDELINES FOR EFFECTIVE PROJECT COMMUNICATION

1. List all the people with whom you will be working. By each name, put *that person's strongest point.* Speak to *that* characteristic. Show each employee that you have confidence in his ability to do the job.

2. Make a *project outline.* Write down the *objective,* the *work needed* to gain that objective, *schedule* (interim and final deadlines), anticipated *problems* and ways to avoid or deal with them. Then do the same for each section of the project that will be run by a different person, adding a section on *instructions.*

3. Schedule time throughout the project for *conferences* with your team—group and individual.

4. Practice giving your instructions and information that you have written in the project outline. Use a mirror and a tape recorder, if possible. Concentrate on giving *step-by-step*

instructions, in *short sentences,* with just *one thought to a sentence.*

5. Before you start a project or go out to supervise one, remind yourself that you are the supervisor, the expert chosen to manage a team of competent, hardworking professionals.

That is your two-phase program for running a project. First you dismiss the fear of chaos by learning all you can about the subject, the project, and the tasks. Once you *know* about each part of the work, you will feel able to *manage* it. Then you prepare to communicate your knowledge and confidence to the other members of your team.

A PROJECT IN ACTION

Let's see how to run a typical on-the-job project. The problem facing you is a piece of major equipment which is proving to be inadequate. This could be a ten-million-dollar computer that doesn't perform all the functions of the latest model. Or it might be a vital production machine. Whatever type of machine it is, the project it engenders is the same.

The project is to determine whether to repair or replace the equipment and how best to do it.

When you're dealing with machinery worth thousands or millions of dollars, you have to devote time and manpower to your decision. A snap judgment may cost you a fortune.

Your responsibility is to find the best solution and put the new or repaired machine to work as quickly as possible. You cannot possibly do all the research and testing yourself. This will be a team project over which you will preside. With authority.

Let's take out a sheet of paper and begin our project.

Map Out The Project. You'll find that the task has two principal parts to it: (1) determining whether to repair or replace the machinery and (2) putting the new or improved equipment to work. Head the first part "Options." List them: (a) Repair old equipment and (b) Replace with new. Under each option, note any *basic* questions you may have. For example:

What is the life expectancy of our present equipment? How long have we had it?

How does it compare to newer models?

Who is using the present equipment?

How much would it cost and how long would it take to repair it?

What possible replacements are there?

What additional benefits would they give us?

How much would each one cost?

Stop when you have the fundamental questions down. You're not trying to do the whole project yourself, now, in your head. You are simply trying to determine what you need to know in order to supervise inquiries.

Now do the same for part two. Make the project manageable for yourself by defining the problems and the tasks involved. You might head this section "Use" and then note:

Who would be using the equipment? For what purposes?

If we buy new machines, what kind of training would we need?

What other uses might we find for the new or repaired machines?

You will be amazed how much better you will feel just after doing this first step! The amorphous project has begun to take shape. An act of drudgery—repairing or buying machinery—is gradually turning into an interesting opportunity to increase productivity. And the project is becoming definitely *yours,* as you size it up, determine priorities, and separate the work into manageable parcels. Now go on to step 2.

Research. See if you can find the answers to your written questions. Check the files for information on your present machine. If your firm has an in-house library, check there for reports on up-to-date competing equipment. If not, go to the public library over lunch or after work. Look under the type of machine in the *Readers' Guide to Periodical Literature.* Check recent issues of pertinent trade magazines. Ask the reference librarian for more sources.

If you know a friendly competitor who uses your present machine or any of the others you're considering, give that person a call. Ask him *briefly* if he's found the equipment satisfactory or if any major problems have come up. Don't, however, become so obsessed with your quest that *you* become a problem! Limit yourself to two or three questions at most.

Now you have done your research. Some of those questions are answered. It's time for step 3.

Set up conferences with proposed project staff. Talk to the people who will help you decide on new or repaired equipment. Also talk to the workers who are using the present machines. Ask your staff to tell you what problems they are having with the machines and what *their* ideas for improvement might be. If you don't understand exactly how the old or new machines operate—and if you *need* to understand in order to make decisions and supervise the study—ask the workers. Don't grill them. Don't try to appear superior—the important boss who usually has far more weighty matters on his mind than the workings of this silly machine. Don't, in other words, try to *justify* your lack of knowledge! Just ask, clearly and simply. Your people will be proud to share their knowledge with you.

Now most, if not all, of your questions should be answered. You can start thinking about dividing the project among your staff. You will be choosing several people to look into the various possibilities. One will find out the merits and demerits of repairing the present equipment. Another will study a possible replacement—say, an improved version of the machine you already have. A third will consider a more elaborate, more expensive machine. A fourth might be responsible for trying out the many possible machines and offering his judgment. Turn to step 4.

Put yourself in the position of each of these project workers. Really imagine that *you* have to go out and do that job. What questions would you have? As the employee studying the possibility of repair, you might ask how many estimates you are supposed to get. How much time you should spend looking. What to test in a sample reconditioned machine.

If you were looking at the new version of the old machine, you might want to know what the company specifically dislikes in the present equipment. You can then check whether those features have been changed or corrected. You would also want to know the production and financial expectations.

How about the job of examining a more sophisticated machine? You would want an idea of the types of jobs the company might be able to give this machine. You would also want to establish a limit on how much the company was willing to spend, so as to know when to stop looking!

And if you were the one slated to test all the possible machines, you would clearly want to know what criteria to apply. Ease of operation? Amount produced? Quality of product? Number of people required to operate machine?

Be aware of these likely questions, and be ready to answer them.

By now, you're going to feel like the number one expert in oscilloscopes, or whatever machine you're handling. Don't deceive yourself —you're not! But you are being a number one boss. You're preparing yourself to give your employees the knowledge, guidance, and support they need.

You've almost, but not quite, completed phase one—the acquiring of relevant knowledge. Step 5 remains.

Take the information you have and check it out with an expert. For this project, your boss would be appropriate. Tell him what you have found out about the present equipment, what sorts of options you are considering, and what criteria you plan to use (cost, productivity, ease of operation, etc.). Ask him if he thinks you should add or correct anything. If he has a suggestion or even a criticism, note it. *Don't* try madly to justify your own criteria or deductions. You have come to him to complete your information, not to impress him with your efficiency. He will respect you far more than if you tried to *make* him respect you!

And now you have the knowledge you need to get to work. You are going to feel wonderful! Just a few logical efforts have made you perfectly comfortable supervising a project about which you knew very little indeed a short time ago. You will feel that you can run this show. And you can.

Now all you have to do is communicate your confidence and knowledge to your staff.

List and assess participants. List the people who will participate in the project. By each name, put that person's strongest point. Let's say Joe Smith is going to look into the advisability of repairing the machine. Write "Joe Smith—*perseverance*" if his greatest asset is that he sticks at a job, or "Joe Smith—*inventiveness*" if inventiveness is his greatest asset. Do this for each project member.

You will make two important discoveries. First, you will find yourself looking for qualities that will help that person do the job you plan to assign him. When you find the appropriate quality, you will know how to present the job. By showing your employee that you have chosen him for this particular assignment *because* of his excellence in a certain area, you will communicate your confidence in him. You will also make the job attractive to him, as he will feel he can excel at it. And you will present it to him from a point of view that he understands.

The other discovery is equally important, if

not so positive. You may find that you have miscast your group. Suppose Joe Smith's strongest on-the-job characteristic is *acute attention to details.* This quality will not impede him in his survey of repair possibilities—but neither will it make him shine. *Inventiveness* could help him a lot, as he might discover cheaper, more effective ways to get the machine back in working order. But Joe is not particularly inventive. He's a good, reliable worker who won't leave a job until every detail is clarified.

That characteristic makes him an ideal candidate for the job of comparing the possible replacements. Joe will check everything. He will test each machine methodically and without bias. That is the job for which you should slate him.

You have given yourself the opportunity to find the best person for each task *before* the event. If you had not taken the time to do this little character test, you would have found out your mistake after you had made the assignments. Then you would have had to face the fact that your initial judgment was wrong—thereby losing a good deal of self-confidence. You might even have had to switch people's jobs in the middle—thereby losing a great deal of goodwill and authority.

Make an outline. Now you can make your *project outline.* This is the document you will use to present the project to your team. For the present job, your outline could look like this:

Project:	To Repair or Replace X Machine and Put the New Machine to Work
Objective:	To find the machine that offers the greatest productivity at a cost of no more than $____
Schedule:	Decision on type of machine to use to be made no later than Sept. 10.
	Reports from researchers to be made to me by Sept. 5. Meeting to discuss findings Sept. 7.
	New or repaired machine to be installed by _____ (to be filled in when we get schedule from installers).
	Machine users to be trained by _____ (ten days after given in-

stallation date, to allow for delays).

Machine to be operating at full efficiency by _____ (five days later). Review of machine, with discussion of user comments or problems _____ (one month later).

Possible problems: Time. Each researcher must schedule his work around this project, delegating some to other workers. Make detailed schedule plan with each team member.

Knowledge. Researchers should have basic understanding of machine's workings and the options available. Give them copies of the research I've done.

Loss of perspective. Each researcher may feel he has to "push" his findings. He may think he has failed if his is not the solution adopted. He may also think he will gain prestige and responsibility if his is the alternative that we decide to take. Make clear that this is a fact-finding mission, that the goal is increased productivity at reasonable cost, and that what will be most appreciated is an unbiased presentation of the pros and cons of each option.

Do a similar outline, more schematic if you like, for each section of the project to be run by a separate person. Add to it any specific instructions you wish to give.

Schedule Meetings. Now there's just one more document. Your calendar. Write on it at least *one morning or afternoon a week when your team members can schedule appointments* to discuss their studies and findings with you, personally. These sessions may be as short as five minutes —but they're vital to a smooth-running operation that remains under your control.

And now you've got it! You have all the knowledge you need to put this project in motion; you've made all the plans you need to have at the start and you have allowed for contingencies. Having recognized, on paper, that problems can and probably will arise, you'll find they won't catch you off guard. Even if they're not the ones you anticipated. Why? Because you have approached this project with a positive, interested attitude. You're ready to roll with it, but you know you'll never have to lose control.

Your staff will know it, too, as soon as you walk into the conference room with your notes, your copies of background material, and your positive attitude. Just to be sure you feel comfortable explaining the project to them— *take time now to practice.*

Practice presentation. Use a mirror and a tape recorder, if they don't make you uncomfortable. Concentrate on making your presentation clear, concise, and interesting. Use short sentences with just one thought to each.

Practice giving your staff a summary of the problem and the project. Simply tell them that your present machine is not functioning well enough for production needs. Outline the options and the advantages and disadvantages of each. Tell them that you need one person to research each option and one to test the proposed machines against each other.

Then go on to tell them who will do what and outline your proposed schedule. When you have outlined the project and the schedule (complete with your slated days for conferences), ask for questions. Try not to have your presentation interrupted by ardent hand-wavers. They can wait until you are ready to turn the floor over to them. You are *not* about to turn your authority over to them!

The final step. You've practiced your presentation. You're ready to get going. Before you call your meeting, however, remember to do the last, important step in preparing effective project communication:

> *Remind yourself that you are the supervisor, the expert chosen to manage a team of competent, hard-working professionals.*

Then you'll communicate both authority and respect.

4
How to Hire a Team of Winners

Men are born to succeed, not to fail.

Thoreau

Now that you feel confident in yourself and in your ability to guide people to do their best, you already have some idea of the types of people you want to work for you. And you can get them. No matter what business you're in or how small your company may be, you can get the best. Because, in one way or another, *you have something to offer that they want and need.*

WHAT PEOPLE LOOK FOR IN A JOB

In September 1983 a three-year study of American work attitudes, conducted by the Public Agenda Foundation of New York, concluded that people work harder if they are given *potential for advancement,* a *chance to develop abilities,* and *a challenging job.*

In the survey of management trainees mentioned in Chapter 1, respondents stated that they sought positions offering *informality, attention to accomplishment, flexibility, independence, community involvement, results orientation,* and *personal interest.*

Another recent study, by the Harvard University Business School, found that employees today want top management to turn its attention to social action rather than profits and costs. The employees also expressed a strong need to be rid of restraints, rules, and pressures that might limit personal freedom.

People *don't* work just for money. You can compete with firms dangling big financial packages by offering *nonfinancial benefits* that people may need more.

YOUR PURSUIT OF EXCELLENCE

Look at the favorite job attributes again: *potential for advancement . . . a chance to develop abilities . . . a challenging job . . . informality . . . attention to accomplishment . . . flexibility . . . independence . . . community involvement . . . results orientation . . . personal interest.*

How many can you already offer? Quite a few, I'm sure, if you put your mind to it. Are there others you could add? Think creatively. You might be able to offer some educational benefits as part of the remuneration. You could entice people with time instead of money, perhaps by making every Friday a short workday. You might set up a babysitting service for people with young children. Discuss your ideas with your superiors to see if they could be fitted into company policy.

In your ad, stress the benefits you offer. Tell the employment agency to describe them to possible recruits. And *realize* that you're offering the right person a great opportunity. Your own conviction will reach out and entice him.

THE RESUME

You have attracted a number of promising candidates by presenting your job effectively. Now—how do you approach them?

Use the resume as a guide. With each resume you get, ask one main question first:

What here suggests that this person could do this job well?

If you can't find a single answer, such as work experience, evidence of leadership, intelligent enthusiasm (in the cover letter), put the resume aside. Ask the question later, after some interviews. Still no answer? Then don't waste the applicant's time and yours.

Next, use the resume as a spur for interview questions. What does the pattern of past employment suggest? Why did the person change jobs so often? What did he get from business school, besides an M.B.A.? Why is he applying for this job? Don't make judgments yet. The resume is only a hazy outline. You need a good personal interview to turn it into a picture.

THE INTERVIEW

The interview is simply *a talk with another person to see if your needs mesh.* Once you accept this equal human relationship, your interview will go well. You will talk honestly with the other person, whose rights and needs you respect. In so doing, you will encourage him to respond in the same way.

You will have a good, revealing talk if you follow the *five strategies of successful hiring:*

1. Clear your mind of all blueprints. Decide on only the essential requirements for the job and make them as general as possible. You want creative, interested people—even if you have to modify your job description somewhat to fit *them.*

2. Look for positive personal qualities as well as technical expertise. You will have to work with the person, not his abilities.

3. Try to hire someone who will complement your present staff. You want neither a whole team of aggressive self-starters nor a bevy of obedient drones.

4. Decide what you will expect of the employee and tell him clearly. See if your purposes and interests match. You will avoid many later disputes and recriminations.

5. Use the interview to amplify and explain the resume. Ask questions that elicit the applicant's attitudes, positive and negative qualities, interests, reasons for applying, and sense of his own abilities. Decide what types of jobs you could comfortably delegate to him. Finally, ask him why he thinks you should hire him over the other applicants.

REFERENCES

If you're really interested in an applicant, call the references he has given you. People are more willing to tell you something personal on the phone than to commit themselves to it in writing. Ask for a general impression of the applicant. Then ask if there's anything special the person could add about him. You may well get specific descriptions and possibly some anecdotes that show you the person on the job.

THE FINAL DECISION

Now that you've formed a personal impression of the applicant, consider four main points:

1. *Competence.* Can he do the job well? *Very* well?

2. *Empathy.* Will he fit the philosophy or culture of our company and our group's character and goals?

3. *Patterns.* Are his patterns of behavior or work acceptable?

4. *Personal rapport.* Did we like each other?

You can't change people. Don't hire someone with the hope that you can. But if your needs match his, you *can* bring out the best in him. That's all you want to do.

5

How to Delegate Work

Because a thing seems difficult for you, do not think it is impossible for anyone to accomplish.

Marcus Aurelius

Once you've got your team together, you can start to delegate work.

It sounds like a dream at first. Getting rid of the busywork. Shifting a few of the responsibilities onto someone else's shoulders. Having more time to devote to the jobs you really want to do.

Until you have to do it.

Then the hesitation starts. You know exactly how to do the job yourself. Wouldn't it actually save time just to *do* it, rather than having to explain it all to someone else? Or—maybe only *this* time you'll do it. Next time you can give it to one of your staff.

DELEGATION WITHOUT FEAR

Delegation is one of the boss's most important functions. After all, one reason you have a staff is because you *can't* do all the work yourself. Your job is to direct, guide, and oversee their efforts—not do their work.

A good boss delegates. A bad boss tries to do it all himself, fails, and then blames everyone else for the poor results. We can all see the logic of delegation, yet we all find it so very difficult. Why?

The answer is fear. We're afraid of losing control of the work. Afraid that it won't be done properly unless we do it. Afraid that it won't be done on time.

Fear of the unknown is natural. It's a tool for our survival. Of course you're afraid of turning over a job whose successful completion is ultimately your responsibility. Your employee is, literally, an "unknown." You don't know whether he can do it . . . how he will approach it . . . what unsuspected difficulties he may have. Your fear is natural. Don't try to deny it or cover it up. It will just fester. Instead, recognize your fear, and then determine not to be ruled by it. How?

First, admit that you are not God. You do not have total control. Not even when you elect to do the job yourself. You could fall ill. A supplier could hold you up. Another project of more pressing urgency could get in the way. Recognize that you can't ever be in complete control—and decide to face whatever happens with a sense of proportion *and* a sense of humor.

Second, stop focusing on the unknown—on what disasters *might* occur. Instead, form a clear idea of *what has to be done* and *how you can facilitate success.*

For any project you will have three *known* goals. You want the job done (1) *well,* (2) *on time,* and (3) *under your control.*

You can make sure the job is done well by giving your employees *clear, explicit instructions, sufficient time and manpower,* and *motivation.*

You can keep your team on schedule by setting up *many short-term deadlines* that you personally supervise.

Let's see how one boss put these principles into practice.

DELEGATION AT WORK

Marilyn is a young entrepreneur who created a successful business by following a simple dictum: Find a need and fill it. She found that working mothers like herself wanted to give their children the nutritional benefits of home-baked snacks. But they had no time to bake them themselves. Marilyn learned how to bake a variety of excellent cookies. She branched out into cupcakes and fruit breads—all made with the best ingredients. Her friends raved. Marilyn set up shop in the suburb where she lived. She hired people to bake the goods, under her strict supervision, and to sell them. She herself took care of ordering supplies and keeping book.

Marilyn's shop was a great success. Marilyn herself was clearly part of it; she was a friendly, people-oriented person who treated her workers well and always greeted the shoppers personally, asking after their families with real interest. She even became known for her creative suggestions for a different birthday or graduation concoction. People grew to depend on her.

One of her customers had a home in Florida. He suggested to Marilyn that she open a shop there. He even offered to invest in it.

Marilyn flew down, looked at the prospect, and agreed. And for the first time faced the need for massive delegation.

She would have to leave her New York shop to set up the business in Florida. She would have to train people in all the areas of running a shop there. This would take at least a month. Her people in New York would have to keep Marilyn's business booming—without Marilyn.

At first she panicked and considered forgetting all about Florida. The New York shop was her personal creation! How could she trust it to anyone else? She didn't even know what she did to make it run. It had all come naturally.

Then her entrepreneurial spirit took over. She could do it. All she had to do was master the art of delegation. Which she did.

First, she decided to make her two salesgirls managers of the shop while she was away. She postponed her trip to Florida in order to have a full month to prepare them. During this time, she showed them how each part of the business was run—from setting up baking schedules to ordering supplies to keeping book. She had them perform each task, under her supervision. Throughout, she expressed her confidence in their abilities.

After the month of exposure and preparation, she asked them what areas of the business still confused or worried them. One girl mentioned the contact with customers. Although Marilyn's clients knew and liked both girls, they had come to depend on Marilyn for party ideas. Marilyn spent that night thinking up ten possibilities for each major holiday. She typed these up, gave them to the girls, and asked them to add their own. They were pleasantly surprised at their own creativity. Marilyn suggested that they put each customer's name by the cake or cookies chosen, so as to cause no duplications of a "custom-made" festival.

Realizing that the two girls could not run the shop and function as full-time salesgirls, Marilyn hired two temporary assistants to work while she was in Florida. She trained these workers both in selling and in ordering supplies, so that they could be of help when needed.

Finally, she closed the shop for a full day, which she devoted to a "dress rehearsal." She play-acted all different types of customers, rigged up imaginary difficulties with suppliers, pretended to burn five batches of cookies, and so on. Just she and her two new managers were there, and their job was to cope with each of these possible disasters. Marilyn conducted the rehearsal with amusement and panache, and the three had fun. The two managers learned by trial, error, and instruction—and ended the day feeling they could handle anything. A good way to start.

Marilyn then gave them their instructions.

She asked them to make a short report of sales, requests, and problems at the end of each day. She would call each morning before the shop opened to receive this report. She also gave them her Florida number and urged them to call any time they needed her help.

She prepared a work plan that gave them alternating jobs. One day one would supervise the baking while the other tended the store; the next day they would switch. This way, they checked each other's mistakes, and no serious problem could be swept under the rug.

Next, she gave them a detailed schedule. So many chocolate chip cookies were to be baked and wrapped by 10 A.M. and 3 P.M. Supplies were to be checked at 2 P.M. every day. And so on. She took a copy of the schedule with her and planned to refer to it in her daily calls.

She arranged to make a trip to New York every Friday to meet with her staff, help them iron out any problems, and maintain the power of her presence.

She called all her staff together to explain how the shop would be run while she was away, including the schedule and the work plan. She asked for and answered everyone's questions.

Finally, she gave her new managers an immediate raise and promised them a further increase on her return, provided they ran the shop according to her instructions. She also told them they would have first chance at running the shop in Florida if they performed well.

The hard work Marilyn devoted to delegating responsibilities in the New York shop had a double payoff. First, she could concentrate on setting up the new business in Florida without worrying about possible problems in New York. Second, her New York shop provided a perfect model for the way to run the Florida business *in absentia*. She had learned how to play, explain, organize, and delegate work in a safe, controlled environment where she felt at home. Now she could apply her techniques to a new place and new people, without fear.

She did.

Today, Marilyn has a shop in Florida, run by one of her original two New York managers, and the shop in New York, where she still presides. Both are flourishing, and Marilyn is starting to look around for a third venture. She knows she can do it. But she could never have done it alone.

DELEGATION AND YOU

You can be equally successful in delegating tasks if you follow the principles that guided Marilyn.

First, you have to accept delegation itself as a job, particularly when you are giving employees work that they have never had to do before. Marilyn put an enormous amount of time, effort, and money into her delegation. Flying from Florida to New York once a week is a drain on a one-woman business. Hiring and training temporary employees adds still more to the cost. But Marilyn knew that successful delegation was essential for her whole new business endeavor. She couldn't risk jeopardizing her New York shop. She had to invest all the money and time necessary to give her new managers what they needed to run it well.

Secondly, remember that successful delegation depends on thoughtful *anticipation.* Try to give yourself and your employees enough time to prepare for the task and to consider any problems that might arise. The members of your staff should be groomed for jobs of increasing responsibility. This is how you build your department or business. So give everyone as much active exposure to different facets of the work as possible. Take employees with you to conferences and meetings, as well as on problem calls. Give them specific jobs on these occasions—note-taking, writing up orders, setting up appointments. This work will keep them involved in what's going on. Increase their responsibilities. Most of the tasks you will be delegating will be shorter, more routine office duties than the one described. Continuous exposure to different jobs will prepare your staff to be able to step in and take control as needed. Make the atmosphere in your office one of growth, of change, of full-team involvement. Your employees will respond well to the interest and novelty of the work you give them. Show them from the beginning that they will be expected to assume greater responsibilities as they grow in the company, and that they will be rewarded for doing so.

Finally, you must have trust. No amount of planning or scheduling will make up for it. Your employees must be able to trust you to help them, make allowances for their lack of experience, and reward them appropriately. You must trust them to do the best they can with what they have.

WHEN THINGS GO WRONG

It will happen. No matter how clearly you all set your goals or how explicit your instructions are, at some point someone on the staff will goof. And you will have to handle it. Here's how.

First, have a moment with yourself. Consider the problem calmly. Ask yourself:

1. What *exactly* did the employee do wrong?

2. What can be done to correct it?

3. What good things has he done lately?

Answer these questions briefly on a card or a piece of paper. Pocket it.

Then say to yourself:

People can work well only if they feel good about themselves. _____ is a good worker who made this mistake for a reason.

If you repeat these sentences, word for word, they will counteract your instinct to charge off and verbally flatten your erring employee. Your job is to help your people do their best. Even when they bungle it.

Now see your employee *alone,* preferably in his office. Calling him to yours may terrify him and make him unable to hear you. Show him immediately that you consider him a worthwhile person who's made a mistake—not a hopeless fool who can't do anything right. Demonstrate that you are criticizing a single error he made, *not* the employee himself, by referring to the good things he's done lately (number 3 on your card). Then tell him exactly what he's done wrong (number 1). Say you want to discuss it with him so that it doesn't happen again.

In this way, you will show the employee that you're displeased with his specific action or nonaction—not with him. You feel he *can* do it properly, if some present obstacle is removed. You're there to help him remove it.

Now it's his turn. Ask him *what went wrong*—and listen to him. If he indicates that your instructions were not clear or that you set unrealistic deadlines for him, consider this information dispassionately. If he's right, admit your part in the problem and tell him to ask you for clarity in the future and to tell you if the schedule is too tight.

If his reasons for failure are personal problems, friction with other employees, or simply a momentary lapse, ask him if he thinks he can resolve the difficulties with or without your help. Help him if he needs it; believe him if he says he can do it alone.

If this problem is one of many, consider

moving the employee to another spot in your organization where his character and abilities would be more appropriate. He may simply be miscast.

Once you've clarified the causes of the problem, discuss ways to resolve it. Give your employee your suggestions (number 2 on your card) and ask him for his. You may find he has a better idea than yours. And by asking him you put him and yourself on the same side. You're two intelligent, mature people facing a joint problem. By this expression of confidence in him, despite his mistake, you make your employee feel able to work hard again.

Your job is always to help your people do the best they can for the company goal. If you concentrate on their strengths, not their weaknesses, and their successes, not their failures, you and they will succeed. Mistakes will become opportunities for furthering understanding instead of reasons to tear out your hair.

THE SEVEN-STEP FORMULA FOR SUCCESSFUL DELEGATION

Follow these seven steps diligently, and you will be able to delegate work without fear or confusion.

1. Anticipate delegation. Give employees as much exposure to as many jobs as possible. After each trial, encourage them to ask questions and to tell you what parts of the job they would find difficult.

2. Prepare. Set aside time to run through instructions. If possible, create a simulation exercise (as Marilyn did by shutting up shop for a day of on-the-job training).

3. Break up the task into manageable segments. You may do a job by instinct or personal whim. That's fine—you're used to it. But when you hand it over to someone else, make it manageable for him. Give him a certain amount to do in a certain time, with a specific, limited objective and a specific report. This method has three advantages. One, it enables you to stay closely in touch with the project, as you receive frequent reports on its phase-by-phase progression. Two, it gives the employee clear goals and limited objectives that he feels he can achieve. Three, it offers the employee frequent opportunities for satisfaction from a job well done and for positive reinforcement from you.

4. Motivate your employees. Obviously, you can't give a raise every time you delegate a small job. Don't forget the nonfinancial rewards. Praise the employee. Take away some of his more onerous tasks while he has the new work to do. Assure him that you are readying him for a position of more authority and responsibility—and mean it.

5. Maintain control by keeping in touch. This means putting yourself out. It doesn't mean cracking the whip. You can maintain a healthy control over the project by giving your staff a series of interim deadlines and setting up discussion time around those deadlines. You can call for short, frequent reports and make sure to convey the findings to your whole team. You can join your employees on the job whenever possible, offering any help they need. *But* —you have to be careful. Remember, you have delegated work to people. If you keep hovering over them, they will wonder why you chose them (since you obviously don't trust them to do it alone) and, furthermore, why you don't continue doing it yourself. They will resent you and lose confidence in themselves. What is the answer? *Attitude.* If you are honestly ready to turn the work over to your employees, they will know it. You can tell them! At the beginning of the project, explain that you have confidence in them, that you are excited about the project, and that you look forward to being a part of it with them. Then your presence will be a statement of your interest, concern, and enthusiasm. But if your attitude is one of mistrust . . . if you feel you've got to supervise every hammer and nail . . . forget about delegating. You're doing it yourself anyway.

6. Set up a system of checks and balances. When we make a foolish mistake, our natural inclination is to cover it up. We do not, as a rule, strain to get to the boss to confront him with it. The trouble is, the mistake is still there. It may lead to further errors or problems, which we first try to sweep away and then accept as overwhelming. You can avoid this pattern on your projects by setting up a system of checks and balances. One way is to have alternating jobs, as Marilyn did. If one employee makes a mistake in the bookkeeping, say, the other is likely to find it when it's his turn to do the accounts. And the second employee doesn't intend to be blamed for it. You, the supervisor, will hear of it before it goes too far. Another way to enable the employees to check each other is to set up frequent discussions between them—without you. You then give them the opportunity to clear up small problems that they may be hesitant to bring to the boss.

7. Don't give people more than they can handle. Imagine yourself in their situation, with their amount of experience and with the work they have to do. It's easy to assume "Joe can do it" when Joe isn't you. Take it as a general rule that you can't add a job to someone's workday without taking away another. If you force him to do both, he will have to do them both half well. When you delegate work, either put more people on one of your employee's jobs or cut back some of his original workload. It's a matter of simple arithmetic!

Now you're ready to delegate fearlessly. Remember, no job is too big for the right number of well-prepared people. And no job is too small to warrant adequate preparation.

6
How to Get Your People to Do Their Best

*The surest plan to make a Man
Is: Think him so.*

James R. Lowell

A business organization is a group of people working together to succeed—as a group and individually—in a particular profession. The person guiding that group is the boss.

The concept is simple and straightforward. But programs and publications of elaborate management theories have muddied it. Educated managers now create *task forces* to determine the accuracy of job descriptions . . . set up *time-and-motion studies* and keep them at a steady whir . . . show recent *M.B.A.'s* how to achieve good *R.O.I.'s* (Returns on Investments) through rigorous *M.B.O.* (Management by Objectives). They call it all a part of *O.D. (Organizational Dynamics)* and justify its complexities by pointing to the sacred goal of another big *O.D. (Organizational Development)*. Then, when employees cry that as people they're being forgotten, the company gives them a shot of *H.R.M. (Human Resources Management)* to make them feel better for a while.

Companies have indeed *OD'd* on personnel management terminology and mini-modules of management training.

We have to forget about "the organization" and think about the people who make it. If you want your people to give you their very best, you've got to give them a reason for doing so. You have to fill their needs. You have to remove their impediments to work. In short, you have to clear the slate of all that heavy, impersonal terminology and go back to the basic, human question: Why do people work?

Then you will know what hinders them in their efforts and how you can help your staff members do their best.

WHY PEOPLE WORK

In 1936, psychologist Abraham Maslow formulated four primary needs that motivate people to work. According to Dr. Maslow, people work to feel:

1. physically contented

2. secure

3. socially accepted or important

4. personally fulfilled

If your work amply fills each of these needs, you will work willingly and hard. But if it does not answer one or more of the four, the unfulfilled needs will get in the way of your performing well. The same, of course, holds for your staff.

You can help your staff members do their best by doing *your* best to fill those four needs for them in the workplace.

Let's take them one by one.

Physical contentment

This first need is the basic one. To feel contented, people need enough food, clothing, shelter, and space. You must offer a salary that enables your employee to secure these material necessities. If your lack of funds or his lack of training makes it difficult to pay him a good salary now, you can offer him a job that will clearly lead to a higher-paying position, either with your firm or elsewhere.

But notice I listed four components of physical contentment—enough food, clothing, shelter, *and* space. People need all four at work, as well as at home—including space. Human beings hate to be boxed in. If you try to save money by cramming two or three people into a single office, you will violate those people's need for space. By denying them this need, you make it impossible for them to perform at their maximum. You may offend and ultimately lose them. And the cost of hiring and training new people would certainly make your space-saving efforts a masterpiece of false economy.

Be conscious of your employees' physical needs. Executives don't get big offices only to establish their importance (though that's part of the reason, and it answers Maslow's need number four). The big office gives them the *space* we all crave. Try to arrange your work area so that each employee has enough space and privacy. If it takes time, explain to your staff what you are trying to do. *Recognition* of their needs goes a long way toward meeting them.

Security

Your employees need to feel secure. They need to know that their jobs are safe. They need to feel that this company is *theirs,* and that management is eager to help them improve their positions there.

To give your staff members security, *tell* them routinely of the company's plans and their place within them. In this way, you will also satisfy the third need—to feel *socially accepted and important* in the company scheme.

There's another way to give your employees security. Let them go—up. Don't hold them back. If one of your staff members has progressed as far as he can go in your department and you think he merits promotion—let him go. It's not easy to give up a star. But *no* good employee will want to work for you if you have the reputation of keeping your people back. Let them know this is their company—a place where they can feel secure about their future, provided they work well today.

Social acceptance and importance

You can speak to this need every working day, as you pause to chat pleasantly with your employees and ask their opinion on matters relating to their work. This basic human contact is so simple and so useful to both of you that you might think all bosses would initiate it naturally. They don't. They think pausing for a talk is either a waste of valuable work time or a spot on their image of unassailable superiority. In this delusion, they lose both the goodwill and the information their employees might have been willing to give them.

You can also make your employees feel socially accepted and important by giving them certain high-visibility jobs. You might have one worker take a visitor around part of the plant, instead of doing it all yourself. You might take another out to lunch with you when you entertain that visitor. You might even ask an employee to explain a project to *your* boss or to an interested client. Of course, all these tasks require effort and trust on your part. It would be easier, and perhaps safer, to do them all yourself, alone. But if you want your employees to shine, you've got to give them the chance and the preparation to do so.

Personal fulfillment

Personal fulfillment implies a sense of accomplishment and meaning in one's life and work. It's the satisfaction of an inner drive that takes different forms in different people. We'll talk about ways to discover your employees' individual needs in a minute. But first, there's one technique you can use on the job that will give all your workers a sense of meaning and personal accomplishment in their work. And it will get the job done.

EMPLOYEE GOAL-SETTING

The technique is goal-setting—with a difference. You don't set the goals. Your employees do.

Every three months, each employee writes down goals for himself for the coming quarter. At the end of the quarter, *he* evaluates the percentage of his achievement. Then he brings you his completed goal sheet for that quarter. For each goal set, it will show:

Goal defined _____

Percentage achieved _____

Other work that interfered with achievement (if any) _____

You should also make goal sheets for yourself. They will bring you the same advantages they give your employees—control of your work, a sense of achievement, the challenge of meeting your own expectations. And they will help you understand your employees' difficulties in *meeting* their goals.

This is how you prepare a goal sheet. Use these guidelines to teach your employees, as well as to do your own.

• Write goals for that three-month period only.

If you think you can complete only one eighth

of a project that quarter, write down "one eighth of project X." Describe exactly what you hope to achieve. Don't fudge or exaggerate. This is for *you*.

• Write goals whose completion depends on no one but you.

Suppose one project is to transfer goods from one building to another. One employee's job is to supervise that transfer. He must order and check an inventory of the goods before and after the transfer, and he must contact the transportation people. Now, as a goal, he should *not* write: Transfer goods from Building A to Building B. Why? Because he has no control over the transporters' schedule or efficiency. That goal would depend on them as much as on him. He should write exactly what he can do:

    Project—Transfer of goods from A to B
    Goals: (1) Order inventory of goods in A
           (2) Supervise inventory
           (3) Contact transporters to set up transfer
           (4) Supervise transfer
           (5) Order inventory of goods in B after transfer
           (6) Supervise inventory

By making the goals specific, limited, and feasible, the employee can more easily keep track of the project's progress. He can pinpoint problems as they arise. And he can feel the satisfaction of accomplishing each goal.

- Write goals that are realistic but that stretch you.

Realistic goal-setting comes with experience. Here's the formula. Your goal should be such that:

1. You can achieve 85–90 percent with reasonable effort.

2. You can achieve 100 percent with maximum effort and some luck.

If you find you're regularly achieving less than 75 percent of your written goals, you're being overambitious and unrealistic. And if you're achieving 100–125 percent you're playing it safe and not stretching yourself enough.

- Under each goal, leave a space for "Other Work."

If you don't achieve a goal, note the other work that prevented you from doing so. You will soon see whether you budgeted your time correctly or whether you could improve on your daily schedule and your ability to allow for unforeseen events. Even more important, you will *understand* why you didn't meet your own objectives. Understanding will take the place of self-justification or guilt—two useless, debilitating responses to an imagined failure.

- Never change the wording of a goal once the quarter begins.

You don't change the rules of a game while you're in it. If you secretly alter your objectives as you fear you won't meet them, you'll rob yourself of control and understanding of your work and of the personal pride in honest accomplishment. (You can check this step for your employees by keeping copies of their goal sheets at the beginning of each quarter. Do the same for yourself!)

At the end of each quarter, discuss the goal sheets and their results with your employees. If you feel their assessment of their performance is inaccurate, correct it. Experienced managers who regularly use this goal-setting technique have found that the changes they made were almost always *up*. People don't tend to overestimate themselves on paper—particularly if their boss is going to see their assessment. So—think before you tell an employee he has exaggerated his success. You may be needlessly damaging an ego. If he keeps failing, his results will show him better than you can.

PERSONAL FULFILLMENT AND FREEDOM

Employee goal-setting is an excellent technique for motivating people to complete their work well while giving them a sense of personal accomplishment. It will certainly improve the productivity and goodwill of your workers. But it is not all there is to personal fulfillment.

For some workers, fulfillment implies personal and professional freedom and other values that neither money nor interesting work can secure.

I know of a manager who is still in shock over the behavior of one of his most valued subordinates, David G. David was an excellent, creative worker who approached his job with interest and freshness, always willing to give a little bit more to a project or to try a new way, even if it meant more work. He was a perfectionist, an achiever. But one day he sent his boss spinning. He actually turned down a substantial raise and promotion. A few days later, David appeared before his boss's desk with a proposal of his own. He was glad the company wanted to reward him for his work—

but he didn't want a raise or a promotion. Instead, he said he would continue to work for the same salary. He would guarantee the company 35 hours of work a week, 50 weeks of the year. The only change was, he would work from home. He would come into the office only when absolutely necessary. He promised to meet all his deadlines, as he always had, and assured his boss that he would be available at home from nine to five, every day.

If the company could not see its way to rewarding him in this novel way, David said, he was sorry, but he would have to resign. He was known for his fine work, and he had already built up enough contacts to start a freelance business of his own.

But why work from home? his manager asked, wide-eyed. In his 35 years of work experience he had never heard anything that sounded to him so preposterous. To turn down a raise and a promotion in favor of—diaper changes? (David's wife had just had a baby.) Dirty dishes? Domestic doldrums?

David smiled. You could put it that way, he answered. Their baby was now two weeks old, and he wanted to be there "to watch my daughter grow up."

David was too good to lose, and he got his

wishes, with some variations. His boss is still shaking his head.

David's decision reminded me of a similar one made by a friend of mine some years ago. He was a director of research at a small electronics firm. One day he was approached by a much larger corporation with an offer to join them as vice president of research at a salary increase of nearly 50 percent. My friend said no. He told me he didn't like "the character" of the larger firm. It was aggressive, engulfing, and extremely profit-oriented, and its people, according to my friend, were "re-shaped and re-oiled every morning to fit into the machine and keep it racing." My friend's small company treated him with great respect and gave him both scientific and budgetary freedom in his lab. These job assets were worth more to him than the more impressive salary and title offered by the other firm.

As a good boss, you must learn to identify what each staff member needs in order to work well. Then you can decide whether you can meet these needs—and whether you are willing to do so. If you're not, chances are your employee will never do his best for you.

DISCOVERING YOUR EMPLOYEES' NEEDS

What does each member of your staff need to feel personally fulfilled?

One good way to find out is to have frequent, informal conversations with each employee. These should not be billed as "business conferences." They are simply chats. Casual, one-to-one discussions about the job. You might ask a staff member to have a cup of coffee with you one morning, or a light lunch. You might ride home from work with an employee. If no social opportunity arises, just drop into your employee's office and sit down for a talk. Once you establish these chats as part of your working routine, your employees won't fear that you're out to grill them or that their jobs are on the line. They will look forward to talking with you about their work.

Talk openly with your employee. Ask him what he likes and dislikes about his job. Ask him if he has any problems he'd like to discuss with you. Try very hard to be sensitive to the feelings revealed by his responses. You'll be surprised at how much you learn.

Are you starting to balk at this? Is a voice inside you grumbling, "I'm not here to 'understand' or 'counsel' my people. I'm here to get them to do their job!"

My answer to that voice is, "You're right. And this is the way to get them to do it."

The aim is not to kill yourself by attempting to accede to each employee's every whim. Rather, you are trying to *learn* what your staff members need and what may be hindering them from doing their best. If you can fill their needs, they are much more likely to fill yours.

REWARDS TO MATCH NEEDS

If I'm an ardent skier who can't swim, and you send me to Barbados in the winter as a "reward" for my fine work, I'll thank you. But I'll be wishing you had asked me where *I* would have liked to go.

Instead of automatically doling out certain rewards—such as upgrading a job title or even giving an employee a small merit raise—think first. Think about the particular needs you discovered in your discussions with your workers. Ask yourself if you're giving a reward that matches a great need. If you're not, it's not that much of a reward. And the unanswered need will remain a steady hindrance to the employee's effective work for you.

Try to find rewards that fill each employee's unspoken definition of personal fulfillment. Suppose you have discerned that a certain employee needs outward acknowledgment of his successes. He needs to feel that the world knows he's tops. We all do, of course—but this employee needs recognition more than, say, independence or free time. He *has* to be clearly praised if he is to feel fulfilled.

You can reward this employee for good work with what some call "psychic income": income that boosts your ego rather than your bank balance. Examples of psychic income are:

- a letter from the company president, commending the employee on his fine work

- a new, larger, more luxurious office

- an invitation to dinner at your home

By rewarding this employee according to his needs, you will make him proud and happy to work for you. The extra psychic income you give him may actually be worth more to him than money in the bank.

Other people with different definitions of personal fulfillment appreciate different types of rewards. Some would prefer independence to a bigger office. Look at David G. and my friend in the electronics firm. These two are not atypical. Many creative people who enjoy their work and often excel at it need to feel free in order to work well. Such people prefer "freedom rewards." Freedom rewards include:

- early time off with pay

- extended breaks and lunch periods

- personal time off with pay

Recent studies have shown freedom rewards to be extremely effective in increasing employee productivity. But many bosses don't like them. Their attitude is: I pay for eight hours and I want eight hours of work.

My question to them is: Are you sure you're paying for eight hours of work? Or are you paying an employee to do the best job he can do for you, on schedule?

If you reward an excellent worker by giving him a shorter workday, and he continues to produce top quality work on schedule, what is there to complain about? If you have the niggling doubt that he might be giving you two more hours of top work if you *hadn't* cut back his day to six hours, forget it. He's staying with you and working to his utmost for you because you have given him an appropriate reward.

Six hours of excellent work is better than eight hours of mediocrity. Depending on the employee and the job, free time is definitely a viable reward.

Of course, money is sometimes the reward your employee needs, wants, and deserves. Still, you can give this reward in effective or ineffective ways. The study of American work attitudes conducted by the Public Agenda Foundation found that 61 percent of American workers want "pay tied to performance" more than any other feature of their work. Only 22 percent see any direct relationship between the quality of their work and the amount on their paycheck. And 73 percent admit that their effort on the job has declined as a result.

All rewards should be earned; otherwise, they cease to be rewards. The employee should clearly understand that you are giving him a raise because he performed so well. The interval between the performance and the reward must be short enough to establish this connection.

Use raises to show your employees that you appreciate their hard work. The raise can be a substantial proof of your appreciation and their worth—if it's given at the right time and accompanied by verbal recognition.

Think carefully about the four reasons people work. Consider them in all your dealings with your staff. If you treat each staff member with honesty, respect, and care, *you'll* be well rewarded.

7

How to Be
the Best Boss

I am larger, better than I thought,
I did not know I held so much goodness.

Walt Whitman

By now, I hope you have seen that being a boss can be tremendously exciting—if you work at it. Being a boss is a job in itself: the job of orchestrating disparate talents to produce harmonious, effective results.

This book has given you techniques for hiring the right people, managing them, delegating work to them, and stimulating them to do their best. If you follow these techniques rigorously and regularly, you will succeed as a boss. You will have a department or business where both productivity and goodwill run high. People will enjoy working for you—provided you take the time for them.

But—you have other jobs, besides managing your staff. Like making budgets. Or setting up production schedules. How can you have the time and energy you need to run your department with all these other diverse responsibilities laying claim to your attention?

First, you have to take time to make time.

YOUR RESPONSIBILITIES

Determine *right now* to set aside an evening or a weekend afternoon soon, to see what your responsibilities are and how best to meet them.

At that time, make a list of your responsibilities. Here's a sample; you may add or delete specific duties according to your needs.

Responsibilities

Legal

Know and inform staff of all legal restrictions on our work, including:

> Antitrust
> Safety
> Environmental Control
> (other)

Safety

Be sure workplace is safe. Establish safety guidelines. Monitor plant regularly to check on possible hazards to safety. Make up a safety checklist to be filled out monthly.

Product

Check product warranties and our responsibilities to the customer. Explain them to all staff members. Keep self and staff up to date on changes.

Budgets

Write semiannual or annual budget. Institute quarterly reviews to see if we're meeting our budget, and if not, why not. Submit budget for approval.

Production Schedules

Make long-term, monthly, weekly, and daily schedules. Review them when scheduled period is over.

Delivery Schedules

Again, long-term, monthly, weekly, and daily schedules, followed by review to see if they were followed.

Maintenance Programs

Set up annual and possibly short-term inspections of machinery. Regular preventive maintenance checks to be made monthly. Crisis control:

establish system for dealing with a breakdown.

Education
Read technical literature on our subject. Tell new findings to staff once a month. Check into educational programs that might benefit staff.

DELEGATING RESPONSIBILITIES

Looking at this list and your own variations on it, one word should leap to your mind. DELEGATION. You can delegate each of these tasks to a staff member, following the techniques of delegation given in Chapter 4.

But notice, I said DELEGATION, not ABDICATION. These responsibilities are yours. You must remain in control of them. That means you must know all that is necessary to know in each area. Your employees can gather the facts, make out the schedules, and even implement the plans—but always under your direct supervision and with your complete knowledge.

For example, you can make one employee your "legal representative." He will research the latest legislation on antitrust, safety, and environmental control. If you have access to a lawyer, ask your employee to get the facts from him. If not, send your legal representative to the library. Let him bring his discoveries to you first. Then help him plan a staff meeting to explain them to everyone, and have him follow up the meeting with a memo to be kept for reference. Make it his job to check periodically for changes in the laws. Always have him report new findings to you, first.

You follow this pattern for each responsibility. Ask one employee to take charge of getting and disseminating the information. Let him do the research. You may prefer to join him at preliminary meetings with authorities, such as the lawyer. Then discuss his findings or schedules with him. Prepare them together, so that he can present them to the staff and then put them into action. Be sure he follows his explanations with a memo to the staff. And ask him for regular, periodic reports on new information or company progress in following his schedules or guidelines.

Of course, handling these responsibilities will be a fair amount of work for your employee, especially at the beginning. After a while, he'll know where to look for information and how to set up schedules or data sheets. But be sure to relieve him of some other job when you delegate this work to him.

There are some jobs you can't delegate—

such as your own professional work, reports to your boss, or certain meetings and conferences you have to attend. By delegating the other tasks, you will give yourself the time and energy you need for these important jobs that only you can do. But—there is still a danger. You may tend to put these other jobs ahead of your daily attention to your employees.

FOCUSING ON YOUR STAFF

If your boss asks you to make out a report, or go to a meeting, or attend a conference—you'll do it when he asks, if not sooner. If an important client shows up for a tour and a lunch with you—you'll be at his service.

But your employees aren't in a position to give you any orders or crack any whips. And that makes them so easy to ignore.

Your staff can be your most valuable asset— or your greatest possible liability. Don't ever forget that. If your people are honest and if they willingly work hard for you and for themselves, you will be successful. But if people in your employ start to cheat you or each other . . . if they slack off on their work . . . if they keep leaving, and you have to keep re-hiring—*you* will suffer, no matter how well you respond to your boss's or your clients' requests.

You cannot afford to ignore any member of your staff. Your daily dealings with your employees are every bit as important as the seemingly bigger events in your worklife—entertaining a prospective customer, making a report to your boss, investing in a new, expensive machine. Neither the customer nor the machine can really make or break you. Your staff can.

To be sure you regularly give your staff what they need to work well for you, add another category to that RESPONSIBILITIES list. One that you cannot delegate. Head it STAFF. Then write down the name of each of your employees. Whenever you hire someone new, add his name to the list.

This list of responsibilities should have a special place in your desk. Better yet, make twelve copies of it and place one before each calendar month. You should refer to it once a month, *every month,* to be sure you're on top of all those responsibilities. When you come to STAFF, ask yourself two questions for each member:

1. Have I taken time to chat casually with _____ about his job, at least twice this month?

2. Have I had occasion to reward him for work done well some time over the past two months?

Then, for the staff as a whole, ask yourself: Have we had an informal meeting every week this month?

WEEKLY MEETINGS

Unstructured rap sessions are the best way to remind you of the presence, needs, and personalities of your staff members. The meetings also form an excellent antidote to the very structured, goal-oriented lives we lead in business.

People have to know and enjoy each other if they are to work well together. They must also feel free to air their feelings and their frustrations, in a nonjudgmental setting.

In his book *Synergistic Management,* Michael Doctoroff describes how these informal meetings helped carry his department over some difficult, tension-filled times. The meetings enabled people to rid themselves of their worries by sharing them. Gradually, they worked them out together.

Doctoroff established some simple, effective rules for the weekly meetings. Only the boss and his immediate staff were to attend. No one was to chair the meeting. There was to be no agenda, no note-taking, and no reporting to superiors or subordinates. The meetings were to last only one hour.

Under these conditions, people felt free to express themselves honestly and without constraints. Both the boss and his staff looked forward to the meetings and always felt better after them.

Are you worried about giving up an hour a week? Then hold your informal meetings every other week to start. My bet is that you'll soon double them. Sometimes more problems are resolved and more new ideas aired during that unstructured hour than during a whole week of work!

THE PYGMALION EFFECT—OR WHY MEETINGS WORK

In George Bernard Shaw's *Pygmalion,* Eliza Doolittle complains to Colonel Pickering:

. . . the difference between a lady and flower girl is not how she behaves but how she is treated. I shall always be a flower girl to Professor Higgins, because he always treats me as a flower girl, and always will; but I know I can be a lady to you, because you always treat me as a lady, and always will. (*Pygmalion*, Act V)

Professor Higgins has worked solidly to change Eliza's speech and manners. But she expresses a truth he had never considered. She will never fully become the lady he wants her to be until *he treats her as that lady*, not a flower girl in masquerade.

Eliza is teaching the professor the Pygmalion effect: one person *can* give another new life—new abilities, new skills—but only by believing in him and treating him as if he already had those abilities and skills.

The Pygmalion effect works powerfully in business. As a boss, you can literally give your employees new life, as you help them stretch to the utmost of their capabilities. Recent studies have shown that:

- Employees' performance and career progress are *directly determined* by their bosses' expectations and treatment of them

- If a boss sets feasible high-performance goals for his staff, the staff generally meets them

In other words, the quality and amount of work people do reflects the quality and amount of *attention* and *confidence* they receive.

Conversely, the studies showed, bosses who treat their staff as unmotivated, lazy under-achievers end up with a group of people who are just that.

Think about your staff for a minute. How do you see each one of them? Do you believe he can do what you ask of him? Have you consciously tried to communicate your confidence in him to him?

The Pygmalion effect reflects the need we all have to be recognized as *special*. Remember Maslow's need number three—to be socially accepted or important. People feel they can do marvels if you, their boss, show them that you think they can. You can't do that if you ignore them.

Periodic, formal expressions of appreciation, such as positive performance reviews or salary increases, are not enough to keep your employees' spirits and performances up. Those regular chats and weekly meetings, during which you express sincere interest and approval, will show your employees that you consider them worthy of your most valued possession: your time.

THE PROBLEM OF NEGATIVE RECOGNITION

It's strange, but the evidence proves it's true: human beings prefer *any* recognition—even criticism—to none at all. The adage "the only bad publicity is no publicity" seems to apply to us all, not only those of us in show business. Criminals have gone on record stating that the reason they broke the law was to be noticed. Human beings, it appears, cannot bear neglect.

Recently, industrial psychologists have discovered that employees will actually do poor work on purpose, in the hope of being reprimanded. Unbelievable? But true. A reprimand is recognition, albeit negative. It's bad publicity, if you like. But it beats no publicity at all.

People need to be noticed.

Now you can see how misguided the complacent boss is, the one who claims proudly "I leave my people alone so long as they do their work." He is starving his people of recognition. He pays attention to them only when they *don't* do their work. And some of them will eventually make noticeable mistakes—just to be noticed.

The Pygmalion effect comes from positive recognition. Pay attention to your employees. Show them that you see them as capable, even exceptional, workers. You will answer their need to be recognized, and they will pick up and reflect your positive feelings about them. Soon they will develop the confidence they need to excel.

By instituting chats and informal meetings with your staff, you will be sure to give them regular attention and recognition. The other way to provide positive recognition is to ask for their opinions and suggestions. Set up a departmental suggestion box, if you don't have one. When an employee makes a mistake, ask *him* to offer a remedy. Listen to him. Listen to all your employees' suggestions, requests, opinions, and complaints.

Think back over the last few weeks. Do you know what your employees have been telling you? Have you really listened?

BEING A GOOD LISTENER

All the meetings, chats, and innovative management techniques in the world won't make you into the great boss you want to be—and *can* be—if you don't *listen* to your people. A so-called chat may actually be nothing more than a monologue—yours if you're just telling your employee what he should be doing, his if he is talking and you aren't listening. It's the same with the weekly meetings. Nobody else there may be listening. They may all want to talk. But you, the boss, must listen. You want to know what's really happening in your business —what people's work problems are—where tensions are growing—where you need to give guidance.

Do you listen when someone is talking to you? Or are you either planning what to say next or reacting to a single remark made by the other person? Think about it. Most people, when they are supposedly listening, are doing one of those two things. Consequently, the conversation is full of misunderstandings and resentments.

The real listener is a prized rarity. Reflect for a moment on the people you know whom you deeply respect and the bosses you've had who have brought out the best in you. You will find they are all good listeners. They *want* to understand you. They in turn grow through understanding.

You can be a real listener. It is your final step in becoming a number one boss. Here's how.

First, you must realize that a conversation only takes place when each person *understands* and *is understood by* the other. That means the listener has to put in as much effort as the speaker. When you speak, you concentrate on speaking in a way the listener can understand. When you listen, you concentrate on understanding *all* that the other person is telling you.

That dimension alone—to focus on understanding, not reacting or preparing to speak— will start the conversation ball bouncing between you. You'll find your interest and willingness to understand are infectious. Then you can put the following five listening skills into practice.

1. Focus on the speaker. Look directly into his eyes. Listen to his words. Resist the temptation to react to one thing he says and then ignore the rest of it.

2. Listen. When the other person is talking, just listen. This is not as easy as it sounds. We always think we know what the other person is about to say. Sometimes we do—but that's not the point. A conversation is not only a sharing of information. It is a social act during which people try to *understand each other.* You may know *what* the other person is going to say —but do you know *why* he is going to say it? Do you really understand how he feels about it? What makes him think that way? Why he is eager to say this to you? You won't be able to receive his full message unless you concentrate on listening to him.

3. Be open to nonverbal communication.
Open your eyes and your mind to the tone of
the speaker's voice, the expressions on his face,
and the position and gestures of his body. Suppose he is saying, "I'll call him first thing in the
morning." Depending on his tone of voice and
emphasis, he may mean:

I will do it—you don't need to get involved
(I'LL call . . . *said firmly*)

I always have to do everything (I'LL call . . .
said with irritation)

He's the one to approach now (I'll call HIM
. . . *said with determination*)

I'm going to let him have it! (I'll call HIM . . .
said with anger)

I'll do it—but not today (I'll call him FIRST
THING IN THE MORNING *said firmly*)

This is exciting—I look forward to getting on
with it (I'll call him FIRST THING IN THE
MORNING *said with enthusiasm*)

Body gestures, position, and facial expression will either intensify or contradict the impression you receive from the tone. Study
them to assess what the speaker really means.
The words alone are not enough. If you don't

listen to the other messages he's giving you, you may never understand what he really means or what he intends to do.

4. Test your deductions. Tell the speaker what you think he said. Simply say something like "You mean . . ." or "As I understand it, . . ." Remember, you're testing your understanding—you're asking to have it corroborated. You're *not* reacting. So if your *voice* says, "This is what I understand you to say, and it confirms my impression that you are a nincompoop"—you have failed at listening. Your interlocutor will react to that message in your voice, without telling you what he meant, and communication will cease.

5. Respond to the whole message. If the speaker was saying "I'll call him if you want me to, but I'd rather not"—respond to both parts of his message. You might thank him for his offer and then either ask him why he doesn't want to call or offer to do it yourself. Or find a compromise. However you respond, respond to the whole message.

Take these five steps consciously. Soon they'll become automatic. You'll find your communications are much more satisfactory when you learn to interpret people's whole messages correctly. Not just your employees'—

your bosses' and your clients' as well. And as you become a better listener, you'll find people will start listening to you, too.

A GOOD BOSS—YOU

What is a boss? A good boss?

A person who knows what has to be done and who motivates himself and his people to do it as well as possible. Not a tyrant, a terror, or a tsar.

Remember the seven secrets of being a number one boss:

1. Develop professional expertise

2. Sharpen your communication skills

3. Cultivate enthusiasm

4. Keep an open mind

5. Pay attention to accomplishment

6. Be accessible

7. Respect your staff (Treat your staff as you treat your clients)

They all fall under two headings: *time* and *attention.*

Take the time you need to get the knowledge you need—about your business, your employees, your work, and the jobs you have to delegate.

Give your people the time and attention they need to work well.

The techniques offered in this book will take the chaos out of your busy worklife and enable you to handle each of your responsibilities in a planned, ordered way. They will give you authority over your staff and mastery of time.

And with time and people working readily for you, you can enjoy the successful business you are all working so hard to create!

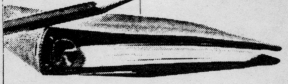